ANOTHER TESTAMENT

ANOTHER TESTAMENT

REFLECTIONS OF CHRIST
MARK MABRY

DESERET
BOOK

SALT LAKE CITY, UTAH

*I dedicate this collection to my sweet wife, Tara, and my three children: Marko,
Bowan, and Ava. Imagining them at the feet of the Savior gives me strokes of
clarity and purpose. And to my youngest son, whom I will meet very soon and
who reminds me that I can love someone whom I haven't yet seen or touched.*

*And to my parents, Mark and Jerri Mabry, who raised me in a place where
I could believe, sent me on a mission, and continue to love me.*

This is for those who would pick up the Book of Mormon and get closer to the Lord.

Library of Congress Cataloging-in-Publication Data
Mabry, Mark.
  Another testament / Mark Mabry.
    p. cm.
  Summary: Photographer Mark Mabry recreates dramatic scenes depicting the visit of Jesus Christ to the Nephite people.
  ISBN 978-1-60641-148-3 (hardbound : alk. paper)
  1. Christian life—Pictorial works. 2. Jesus Christ—Art. 3. Jesus Christ—In the Book of Mormon. 4. Book of Mormon—Illustrations. 5. Portrait photography. I. Title.
  BX8627.M23 2009
  289.3'220222—dc22
                    2009030278

Printed in the United States of America
Inland Graphics, Menomonee Falls, WI
10 9 8 7 6 5 4 3 2 1

PREFACE

My father joined The Church of Jesus Christ of Latter-day Saints when he was eighteen years old. My mother was born a member. I grew up with the Bible and Book of Mormon supporting each other; I naturally looked for the good in both, and I found it. Even today, I continue to find things in the Bible that shed light on what I read in the Book of Mormon and vice versa.

In early 2008, I set out to portray the climax of the Book of Mormon—the appearance of the resurrected Savior to the inhabitants of ancient America. Simple enough, I thought. Producer Steve Porter and I headed down to the jungles of Guatemala, Belize, and Mexico in search of an ancient temple that would fit both our logistic and aesthetic needs. I had spent countless hours studying the story of Christ's appearance to the people of the Book of Mormon. I felt that I could direct the story effectively.

We settled on a location and returned home to the mountainous task of producing the shoot. But while digging into the work, I grew confused. I was uncertain about many aspects. One day I knelt alone by my bed in prayer. My question was simple: "Why is this not coming together?" I figured there was something wrong with the location or my shot selection or something else logistical. This very well could have been the case, but a more pressing answer came clearly and directly, and immediately humbled me.

"You don't know the Book of Mormon well enough."

I prayed more earnestly. "Father, what do I need to know?"

Eventually I realized that the answer existed in the things that weren't spelled out in the text of the Book of Mormon. I felt that the Lord's response to my prayer rested in the moments of the story that were so sacred that they couldn't be uttered or were forbidden to be written (see 3 Nephi 26:16; 28:14).

I began to imagine what could possibly have been done during His visit that was too sacred to have been written or uttered. *Have I ever had a moment like that?* I wondered. *Something too sacred to even write or speak about?* I pondered those questions deeply.

In addition to examining my life in a modern context, I pictured myself living around A.D. 34 as a Nephite near the temple at Bountiful. All of my current fears and faults came with me. Analysis of my life in this light revealed some striking similarities between me and the people of the Book of Mormon.

First, I'm not perfect. Neither were those who were visited by the Lord. We're both trying to follow Christ and we're trying to be humble, but neither I nor they are perfectly successful.

Second, most of the time I believe and show faith. Sometimes I doubt and falter. On special occasions, though, I *know* He lives. That knowledge is a gift that, I believe, can come and go. I'm not claiming to see visions or hear voices, but I'm saying that there is a feeling that is so close to home and to our hearts that it cannot be duplicated by any of our senses. It's a feeling that I know to be the Holy Spirit telling me that the Lord lives and loves me.

The last similarity of note was that those things that were too sacred for Mormon to include in the record took place at the temple. In fact, the only geographic locations mentioned in relation to the Lord's visit were the home, the waters of baptism, and the temple. Likewise, the moments in my life that are too dear to share also have their own sacred spaces. They occur in my home, where we teach our children to pray, repent, and forgive, and where Tara and I work to keep the covenants we've made with each other and with the Lord. Many other sacred moments have happened in the quiet of the modern temple, where my thoughts are broadened and I consider the purpose of my life. I believe the most sacred moments occur when the Lord is speaking to us in a language that is intended for only us, individually.

When all the details for the shoot had been worked out, we decided to use the ruins of Copan in Honduras. Logistically, the location worked. But the logistics ended up being secondary to the experience that we were about to share with the untrained actors who portrayed the events of 3 Nephi chapters 9 through 27.

As the director, I had plenty of questions. How would the people respond to acting out something so sacred? Would there be enough emotion? Would I be able to connect with the people through a translator? Would the whole situation seem weird? Would the cameras be intimidating? Lights? Onlookers? Even if everything went well, would the viewer ultimately be able to connect with the art? I felt immense pressure to deliver something that felt authentic in spite of the unavoidable modern elements of the shoot. The task was daunting.

The first night of shooting was fairly unproductive and few of the images were useable. I felt that my fears were being confirmed. I wasn't connecting with the volunteer actors, and they in turn weren't connecting with the task at hand. The people were stiff as they approached Robert, who was portraying Christ. Kneeling looked painful and forced. I left the shoot that night terrified for the next morning when we were going to portray the initial descent of the Savior and the scene where the people had the chance to go up "one by one" to feel the prints in His hands and feet and side.

It seems as though there are always barriers when a special moment is to be had. For us, the barrier was getting over our knowledge that Robert was a man portraying Christ—he was not really Christ. We all needed to imagine him as a symbol of Christ, the same way we do when we weep in front of a sculpture of Him. How could the cast, crew, and I come to a mutual consensus that it was alright to imagine and portray this situation as being real?

The next morning our crew arrived on set about an hour before the cast. We were alone on the majestic and tragic temple ruins of the ancient Mayans. It was quiet. I retired to a spot around the corner from our set with the intent to pray for help on the shoot. But as I approached the prayer I instead began praying for confirmation that God was hearing my prayer and for the chance to feel the Holy Spirit and to know, if only for a moment, that the Son of God remembers my name. My prayer was answered.

When the cast arrived, I loved them immediately. I felt a change in me. The love was completely natural. We spoke about symbolism and imagination. I noticed tears in a few of their eyes. We were communicating! Norine, Robert's wife, gave a tender example of how she would approach the Savior. Her uninhibited portrayal of a woman meeting the Lord was a sign to others in the cast and crew that it was alright to pretend and imagine for a little bit.

Trusting that the cast was feeling the same way as I was, I stepped back and motioned to them that it was their turn to portray this moment however they wished. The entire cast knelt on the stairs below the platform where Robert was standing. After about thirty seconds, a young man helped his wife to her feet. They approached Robert timidly, with a degree of self-consciousness. Once they were within about a five-foot radius of where Robert stood in his white robe, though, they seemed to forget all about the more than a hundred people watching. The wife examined and kissed Robert's hand. Oteniel, the husband, began to weep and embraced Robert.

The scene continued for some time as nearly the whole group came forward "one by one," letting go of embarrassment and experiencing an individual moment with Robert. The suspension of disbelief from each cast member transformed each photograph into a personal witness that He lives. The crew and I found ourselves longing for the chance to participate in the scene.

Another moment of great anxiety for me was shooting the healing scene. A woman named Lorena had been losing the use of her legs over the last two years. Doctors were unable to diagnose the problem. Lorena moves about with a walker and the assistance of her ever-loyal six-year-old son. The young mother agreed to portray a woman being healed by the Lord. I was concerned that this situation would be awkward. No doubt Lorena has prayed for a scenario in which the Savior touches her and pronounces her healed. Now she was acting out the very scenario of her heart's desire. She was set on Robert's lap. No direction was given. The desire for a good picture was superceded by a wish that this experience could be real. I was worried that it would appear exploitive and callous. It wasn't. All present were moved to tears as she and Robert sat for many minutes wishing and imagining.

The moments we shared on the ruins imagining the Savior's ministry on the American continent are sacred to me. I learned of the power of belief that an entire group of people can generate. I gained even more respect for the God-given power of imagination. It feels natural to me that a God who teaches in symbols would also give His children an innate ability to understand those symbols via the power of imagination mixed with the teaching power of the Holy Ghost.

As the shoot progressed I noticed that this group of people from three different cities had became a group of friends. To me, the most obvious expression of this deepening friendship was among those men who portrayed the chosen twelve disciples of Christ. The images of the twelve men with the Savior tell a story of the ability of the gospel of Christ to deepen friendships instantaneously. At first they were "chosen" but separate, bound together by their calling and assignment. But as the days progressed and they shared in the rapid growth inherent in being taught by the Savior, there was a change in their relationship. The brotherhood that is evident in the photographs of them happened naturally. In fact, the last shot in the series of the twelve disciples was taken candidly, after the intended image was done. These men were hugging and weeping together as friends.

I noticed in my studies of 3 Nephi that the Savior appeared to these people to get things done. From baptism, to giving the gift of the Holy Ghost, to blessing and ministering "one by one," the Savior was interested in the progression of the people involved. I long to know the things that were "too sacred to utter."

It is my opinion and experience that if we ask for those things that are sacred beyond words, God will provide a way for us to receive them. Several of these occasions in my life have happened as I have studied the words of the prophets in the Book of Mormon. I love the Book of Mormon. There are times when I read it that I feel a nearness to the Savior that is both personal and powerful. My most sincere hope for my work with *Another Testament* is that those that view the images will feel compelled to find a Book of Mormon and feel the power of reading and imagining the scenes of these chapters.

From my reading of the Book of Mormon I have gained a love of prophets . . . and a dependence on their insight. Through reading the Book of Mormon and discovering its power, I have concluded that Joseph Smith was a prophet of God and that he not only discovered the Book of Mormon, but also translated it with divine help. I believe that prophets live today and hear the voice of the Lord. This belief gives me hope for the future and another source to turn to for divine guidance.

I love the story of the prophet Nephi III and the people he prepared to meet the Lord. I'm thankful for the ability and opportunity I have been given to share my feelings through photography. I pray that these images can help bring this amazing and sacred story to life and will serve as a tool to enhance our imagination and desire to actually meet Him.

I look forward to the day when I can meet Him and share that experience with everyone that I love.

Will ye not now return unto me, and repent of your sins, and be converted, that I may heal you?

3 NEPHI 9:13

Devastation

And it came to pass in the thirty and fourth year, in the first month, on the fourth day of the month, there arose a great storm, such an one as never had been known in all the land.

And there was also a great and terrible tempest; and there was terrible thunder, insomuch that it did shake the whole earth as if it was about to divide asunder.

And there were exceedingly sharp lightnings, such as never had been known in all the land. . . .

And it came to pass that there was thick darkness upon all the face of the land, insomuch that the inhabitants thereof who had not fallen could feel the vapor of darkness;

And there could be no light, because of the darkness, neither candles, neither torches; neither could there be fire kindled with their fine and exceedingly dry wood, so that there could not be any light at all;

And there was not any light seen, neither fire, nor glimmer, neither the sun, nor the moon, nor the stars, for so great were the mists of darkness which were upon the face of the land.

And it came to pass that it did last for the space of three days that there was no light seen; and there was great mourning and howling and weeping among all the people continually; yea, great were the groanings of the people, because of the darkness and the great destruction which had come upon them.

And in one place they were heard to cry, saying: O that we had repented before this great and terrible day, and then would our brethren have been spared, and they would not have been burned in that great city Zarahemla.

And in another place they were heard to cry and mourn, saying: O that we had repented before this great and terrible day, and had not killed and stoned the prophets, and cast them out; then would our mothers and our fair daughters, and our children have been spared, and not have been buried up in that great city Moronihah. And thus were the howlings of the people great and terrible. —3 NEPHI 8:5–7, 20–25

CHILD OF GOD

Therefore, whoso repenteth and cometh unto me as a little child, him will I receive, for of such is the kingdom of God. Behold, for such I have laid down my life, and have taken it up again; therefore repent, and come unto me ye ends of the earth, and be saved. —3 NEPHI 9:22

MOTHER AND SON

O all ye that are spared because ye were more righteous than they, will ye not now return unto me, and repent of your sins, and be converted, that I may heal you? —3 NEPHI 9:13

. . . *their mourning was turned into joy . . .*

Morning

And it came to pass that thus did the three days pass away. And it was in the morning, and the darkness dispersed from off the face of the land, and the earth did cease to tremble, and the rocks did cease to rend, and the dreadful groanings did cease, and all the tumultuous noises did pass away.

And the earth did cleave together again, that it stood; and the mourning, and the weeping, and the wailing of the people who were spared alive did cease; and their mourning was turned into joy, and their lamentations into the praise and thanksgiving unto the Lord Jesus Christ, their Redeemer. —3 NEPHI 10:9–10

Light and Life

And it came to pass, as they understood they cast their eyes up again towards heaven; and behold, they saw a Man descending out of heaven; and he was clothed in a white robe; and he came down and stood in the midst of them; and the eyes of the whole multitude were turned upon him, and they durst not open their mouths, even one to another, and wist not what it meant, for they thought it was an angel that had appeared unto them.

And it came to pass that he stretched forth his hand and spake unto the people, saying:

Behold, I am Jesus Christ, whom the prophets testified shall come into the world.

And behold, I am the light and the life of the world; and I have drunk out of that bitter cup which the Father hath given me, and have glorified the Father in taking upon me the sins of the world, in the which I have suffered the will of the Father in all things from the beginning. —3 NEPHI 11:8–11

HUMILITY

Arise and come forth unto me, that ye may thrust your hands into my side, and also that ye may feel the prints of the nails in my hands and in my feet, that ye may know that I am the God of Israel, and the God of the whole earth, and have been slain for the sins of the world.

And it came to pass that the multitude went forth, and thrust their hands into his side, and did feel the prints of the nails in his hands and in his feet; and this they did do, going forth one by one until they had all gone forth, and did see with their eyes and did feel with their hands, and did know of a surety and did bear record, that it was he, of whom it was written by the prophets, that should come. —3 NEPHI 11:14–15

EMPATHY

Behold, I have come unto the world to bring redemption unto the world, to save the world from sin. —3 NEPHI 9:21

Return to Me

Nevertheless, ye shall not cast him out of your synagogues, or your places of worship, for unto such shall ye continue to minister; for ye know not but what they will return and repent, and come unto me with full purpose of heart, and I shall heal them; and ye shall be the means of bringing salvation unto them. —3 NEPHI 18:32

SHELTER

O ye people of these great cities which have fallen, who are descendants of Jacob, yea, who are of the house of Israel, how oft have I gathered you as a hen gathereth her chickens under her wings, and have nourished you. . . .

O ye house of Israel whom I have spared, how oft will I gather you as a hen gathereth her chickens under her wings, if ye will repent and return unto me with full purpose of heart. —3 NEPHI 10:4, 6

REACHING

Yea, verily I say unto you, if ye will come unto me ye shall have eternal life. Behold, mine arm of mercy is extended towards you, and whosoever will come, him will I receive; and blessed are those who come unto me. —3 NEPHI 9:14

SURRENDER

And ye shall offer for a sacrifice unto me a broken heart and a contrite spirit. And whoso cometh unto me with a broken heart and a contrite spirit, him will I baptize with fire and with the Holy Ghost. —3 NEPHI 9:20

. . . blessed are the meek . . .

REVERENCE

And blessed are the meek, for they shall inherit the earth. —3 NEPHI 12:5

FIRST INSTINCT

And blessed are all the pure in heart,

for they shall see God. —3 NEPHI 12:8

Little Boys

And blessed are all the peacemakers, for they shall be called the children of God. —3 NEPHI 12:9

Other Sheep

And when they had all gone forth and had witnessed for themselves, they did cry out with one accord, saying:

  Hosanna! Blessed be the name of the Most High God! And they did fall down at the feet of Jesus, and did worship him. —3 NEPHI 11:16–17

. . . they did all go forth and witnessed for themselves . . .

Nephi

And Nephi arose and went forth, and bowed himself before the Lord and did kiss his feet. —3 NEPHI 11:19

Chosen

He stretched forth his hand unto the multitude, and cried unto them, saying: Blessed are ye if ye shall give heed unto the words of these twelve whom I have chosen from among you to minister unto you, and to be your servants. —3 NEPHI 12:1

ALPHA AND OMEGA

Verily, verily, I say unto you, that this is my doctrine, and whoso buildeth upon this buildeth upon my rock, and the gates of hell shall not prevail against them.

—3 NEPHI 11:39

COUNSELOR

Ask, and it shall be given unto you; seek, and ye shall find; knock, and it shall be opened unto you.

For every one that asketh, receiveth; and he that seeketh, findeth; and to him that knocketh, it shall be opened. —3 NEPHI 14:7–8

Yea, blessed are the poor in spirit who come unto me, for theirs is the kingdom of heaven.

And again, blessed are all they that mourn, for they shall be comforted.

And blessed are the meek, for they shall inherit the earth.

And blessed are all they who do hunger and thirst after righteousness, for they shall be filled with the Holy Ghost.

And blessed are the merciful, for they shall obtain mercy.

And blessed are all the pure in heart, for they shall see God.

And blessed are all the peacemakers, for they shall be called the children of God.

And blessed are all they who are persecuted for my name's sake, for theirs is the kingdom of heaven.

And blessed are ye when men shall revile you and persecute, and shall say all manner of evil against you falsely, for my sake;

For ye shall have great joy and be exceedingly glad, for great shall be your reward in heaven;

for so persecuted they the prophets who were before you.

Verily, verily, I say unto you, I give unto you to be the salt of the earth; but if the salt shall lose its savor wherewith shall the earth be salted? The salt shall be thenceforth good for nothing, but to be cast out and to be trodden under foot of men.

Verily, verily, I say unto you, I give unto you to be the light of this people. A city that is set on a hill cannot be hid.

Behold, do men light a candle and put it under a bushel? Nay, but on a candlestick, and it giveth light to all that are in the house;

Therefore let your light so shine before this people, that they may see your good works and glorify your Father who is in heaven.

Think not that I am come to destroy the law or the prophets. I am not come to destroy but to fulfil;

For verily I say unto you, one jot nor one tittle hath not passed away from the law, but in me it hath all been fulfilled. —3 NEPHI 12:3–18

I Perceive

Behold, now it came to pass that when Jesus had spoken these words he looked round about again on the multitude, and he said unto them: Behold, my time is at hand.

I perceive that ye are weak, that ye cannot understand all my words which I am commanded of the Father to speak unto you at this time.

Therefore, go ye unto your homes, and ponder upon the things which I have said, and ask of the Father, in my name, that ye may understand, and prepare your minds for the morrow, and I come unto you again. —3 NEPHI 17:1–3

Bring Them Hither

Have ye any that are sick among you? Bring them hither. Have ye any that are lame, or blind, or halt, or maimed, or leprous, or that are withered, or that are deaf, or that are afflicted in any manner? Bring them hither and I will heal them, for I have compassion upon you; my bowels are filled with mercy. —3 NEPHI 17:7

Rock

For the mountains shall depart and the hills be removed, but my kindness shall not depart from thee, neither shall the covenant of my peace be removed, saith the Lord that hath mercy on thee. —3 NEPHI 22:10

HEALING IN HIS WINGS

But unto you that fear my name, shall the Son of Righteousness arise with healing in his wings; and ye shall go forth and grow up as calves in the stall.

—3 NEPHI 25:2

. . . they did bathe his feet with their tears . . .

MERCY

And they did all, both they who had been healed and they who were whole, bow down at his feet, and did worship him; and as many as could come for the multitude did kiss his feet, insomuch that they did bathe his feet with their tears. —3 NEPHI 17:10

REDEEMER

And when he had said these words, he himself also knelt upon the earth; and behold he prayed unto the Father, and the things which he prayed cannot be written, and the multitude did bear record who heard him.

And after this manner do they bear record: The eye hath never seen, neither hath the ear heard, before, so great and marvelous things as we saw and heard Jesus speak unto the Father;

And no tongue can speak, neither can there be written by any man, neither can the hearts of men conceive so great and marvelous things as we both saw and heard Jesus speak; and no one can conceive of the joy which filled our souls at the time we heard him pray for us unto the Father. —3 NEPHI 17:15–17

ENCIRCLED BY ANGELS

And he spake unto the multitude, and said unto them: Behold your little ones.

And as they looked to behold they cast their eyes towards heaven, and they saw the heavens open, and they saw angels descending out of heaven as it were in the midst of fire; and they came down and encircled those little ones about, and they were encircled about with fire; and the angels did minister unto them. —3 NEPHI 17:23–24

THOSE LITTLE ONES

And when he had said these words, he wept, and the multitude bare record of it, and he took their little children, one by one, and blessed them, and prayed unto the Father for them. —3 NEPHI 17:21

SON OF GOD

And for this cause ye shall have fulness of joy; and ye shall sit down in the kingdom of my Father; yea, your joy shall be full, even as the Father hath given me fulness of joy; and ye shall be even as I am, and I am even as the Father; and the Father and I are one. —3 NEPHI 28:10

Behold your little ones.

Power to Give

And when the multitude had eaten and were filled, he said unto the disciples: Behold there shall one be ordained among you, and to him will I give power that he shall break bread and bless it and give it unto the people of my church, unto all those who shall believe and be baptized in my name.

And this shall ye always observe to do, even as I have done, even as I have broken bread and blessed it and given it unto you. —3 NEPHI 18:5–6

THE BREAD OF LIFE

And he said unto them: He that eateth this bread eateth of my body to his soul; and he that drinketh of this wine drinketh of my blood to his soul; and his soul shall never hunger nor thirst, but shall be filled. —3 NEPHI 20:8

BAPTISM OF NEPHI

And when they had thus prayed they went down unto the water's edge, and the multitude followed them.

And it came to pass that Nephi went down into the water and was baptized. —3 NEPHI 19:10–11

Authority to Baptize

And the Lord said unto him: I give unto you power that ye shall baptize this people when I am again ascended into heaven.

And he came up out of the water and began to baptize. And he baptized all those whom Jesus had chosen. —3 NEPHI 11:21; 19:12

Washed Clean

And it came to pass when they were all baptized and had come up out of the water, the Holy Ghost did fall upon them, and they were filled with the Holy Ghost and with fire. —3 NEPHI 19:13

FAITH

And behold, ye are the children of the prophets; and ye are of the house of Israel; and ye are of the covenant which the Father made with your fathers, saying unto Abraham: And in thy seed shall all the kindreds of the earth be blessed.

The Father having raised me up unto you first, and sent me to bless you in turning away every one of you from his iniquities; and this because ye are the children of the covenant. —3 NEPHI 20:25–26

A NEW LIFE

Enter ye in at the strait gate; for wide is the gate, and broad is the way, which leadeth to destruction, and many there be who go in thereat;

Because strait is the gate, and narrow is the way, which leadeth unto life, and few there be that find it. —3 NEPHI 14:13–14

HE SMILED

And it came to pass that when they had all knelt down upon the earth, he commanded his disciples that they should pray.

And behold, they began to pray; and they did pray unto Jesus, calling him their Lord and their God.

And it came to pass that Jesus blessed them as they did pray unto him; and his countenance did smile upon them, and the light of his countenance did shine upon them, and behold they were as white as the countenance and also the garments of Jesus; and behold the whiteness thereof did exceed all the whiteness, yea, even there could be nothing upon earth so white as the whiteness thereof.

And Jesus said unto them: Pray on; nevertheless they did not cease to pray.

And he turned from them again, and went a little way off and bowed himself to the earth; and he prayed again unto the Father, saying:

Father, I thank thee that thou hast purified those whom I have chosen, because of their faith, and I pray for them, and also for them who shall believe on their words, that they may be purified in me, through faith on their words, even as they are purified in me.

Father, I pray not for the world, but for those whom thou hast given me out of the world, because of their faith, that they may be purified in me, that I may be in them as thou, Father, art in me, that we may be one, that I may be glorified in them.

And when Jesus had spoken these words he came again unto his disciples; and behold they did pray steadfastly, without ceasing, unto him; and he did smile upon them again; and behold they were white, even as Jesus. —3 NEPHI 19:17–18; 25–30

MY JOY IS FULL

And it came to pass that he went again a little way off and prayed unto the Father;

And tongue cannot speak the words which he prayed, neither can be written by man the words which he prayed. —3 NEPHI 19:31–32

OFFERING

And it came to pass that he brake bread again and blessed it, and gave to the disciples to eat.

And when they had eaten he commanded them that they should break bread, and give unto the multitude. . . .

Now, there had been no bread, neither wine, brought by the disciples, neither by the multitude;

But he truly gave unto them bread to eat, and also wine to drink. —3 NEPHI 20:3–4, 6–7

Bring Forth the Record

And it came to pass that he said unto Nephi: Bring forth the record which ye have kept.

And when Nephi had brought forth the records, and laid them before him, he cast his eyes upon them and said:

Verily I say unto you, I commanded my servant Samuel, the Lamanite, that he should testify unto this people, that at the day that the Father should glorify his name in me that there were many saints who should arise from the dead, and should appear unto many, and should minister unto them. And he said unto them: Was it not so? . . .

And it came to pass that Nephi remembered that this thing had not been written.

And it came to pass that Jesus commanded that it should be written; therefore it was written according as he commanded. —3 NEPHI 23:7–9, 12–13

CREATOR

Behold, I am Jesus Christ the Son of God.
I created the heavens and the earth, and
all things that in them are. I was with the
Father from the beginning. I am in the
Father, and the Father in me; and in me
hath the Father glorified his name. . . .

And as many as have received me, to
them have I given to become the sons of
God; and even so will I to as many as shall
believe on my name, for behold, by me
redemption cometh, and in me is the law
of Moses fulfilled. —3 NEPHI 9:15, 17

CONVERTED

And it came to pass that thus they did go forth among all the people of Nephi, and did preach the
gospel of Christ unto all people upon the face of the land; and they were converted unto the Lord, and
were united unto the church of Christ, and thus the people of that generation were blessed, according
to the word of Jesus. —3 NEPHI 28:23

WHITE AS SNOW

Now this is the commandment: Repent, all ye ends of the earth, and come unto me and be baptized in my name, that ye may be sanctified by the reception of the Holy Ghost, that ye may stand spotless before me at the last day. —3 NEPHI 27:20

MARVELOUS THINGS

And it came to pass that he did teach and minister unto the children of the multitude of whom hath been spoken, and he did loose their tongues, and they did speak unto their fathers great and marvelous things, even greater than he had revealed unto the people; and he loosed their tongues that they could utter.

Behold, it came to pass on the morrow that the multitude gathered themselves together, and they both saw and heard these children; yea, even babes did open their mouths and utter marvelous things; and the things which they did utter were forbidden that there should not any man write them. —3 NEPHI 26:14, 16

BROTHERHOOD

Jesus . . . spake unto his disciples, one by one, saying unto them: What is it that ye desire of me, after that I am gone to the Father?

And they all spake, save it were three, saying: We desire that after we have lived unto the age of man, that our ministry, wherein thou hast called us, may have an end, that we may speedily come unto thee in thy kingdom.

And he said unto them: Blessed are ye because ye desired this thing of me; therefore, after that ye are seventy and two years old ye shall come unto me in my kingdom; and with me ye shall find rest.

And when he had spoken unto them, he turned himself unto the three, and said unto them: What will ye that I should do unto you, when I am gone unto the Father?

And they sorrowed in their hearts, for they durst not speak unto him the thing which they desired.

And he said unto them: Behold, I know your thoughts, and ye have desired the thing which John, my beloved, who was with me in my ministry, before that I was lifted up by the Jews, desired of me.

Therefore, more blessed are ye, for ye shall never taste of death; but ye shall live to behold all the doings of the Father unto the children of men, even until all things shall be fulfilled according to the will of the Father, when I shall come in my glory with the powers of heaven.

And ye shall never endure the pains of death; but when I shall come in my glory ye shall be changed in the twinkling of an eye from mortality to immortality; and then shall ye be blessed in the kingdom of my Father.

And again, ye shall not have pain while ye shall dwell in the flesh, neither sorrow save it be for the sins of the world; and all this will I do because of the thing which ye have desired of me, for ye have desired that ye might bring the souls of men unto me, while the world shall stand.

And for this cause ye shall have fulness of joy; and ye shall sit down in the kingdom of my Father; yea, your joy shall be full, even as the Father hath given me fulness of joy; and ye shall be even as I am, and I am even as the Father; and the Father and I are one;

And the Holy Ghost beareth record of the Father and me; and the Father giveth the Holy Ghost unto the children of men, because of me.

And it came to pass that when Jesus had spoken these words, he touched every one of them with his finger save it were the three who were to tarry, and then he departed. —3 NEPHI 28:1-12

. . . that ye do always remember me.

REMEMBER

And this shall ye do in remembrance of my body, which I have shown unto you. And it shall be a testimony unto the Father that ye do always remember me. And if ye do always remember me ye shall have my Spirit to be with you.

And it came to pass that when he said these words, he commanded his disciples that they should take of the wine of the cup and drink of it, and that they should also give unto the multitude that they might drink of it.

And it came to pass that they did so, and did drink of it and were filled; and they gave unto the multitude, and they did drink, and they were filled.

And when the disciples had done this, Jesus said unto them: Blessed are ye for this thing which ye have done, for this is fulfilling my commandments, and this doth witness unto the Father that ye are willing to do that which I have commanded you.

And this shall ye always do to those who repent and are baptized in my name; and ye shall do it in remembrance of my blood, which I have shed for you, that ye may witness unto the Father that ye do always remember me. And if ye do always remember me ye shall have my Spirit to be with you. —3 NEPHI 18:7–11

Excerpt from 3 Nephi

As found in The Book of Mormon: Another Testament of Jesus Christ

CHAPTER 11

1 And now it came to pass that there were a great multitude gathered together, of the people of Nephi, round about the temple which was in the land Bountiful; and they were marveling and wondering one with another, and were showing one to another the great and marvelous change which had taken place.

2 And they were also conversing about this Jesus Christ, of whom the sign had been given concerning his death.

3 And it came to pass that while they were thus conversing one with another, they heard a voice as if it came out of heaven; and they cast their eyes round about, for they understood not the voice which they heard; and it was not a harsh voice, neither was it a loud voice; nevertheless, and notwithstanding it being a small voice it did pierce them that did hear to the center, insomuch that there was no part of their frame that it did not cause to quake; yea, it did pierce them to the very soul, and did cause their hearts to burn.

4 And it came to pass that again they heard the voice, and they understood it not.

5 And again the third time they did hear the voice, and did open their ears to hear it; and their eyes were towards the sound thereof; and they did look steadfastly towards heaven, from whence the sound came.

6 And behold, the third time they did understand the voice which they heard; and it said unto them:

7 Behold my Beloved Son, in whom I am well pleased, in whom I have glorified my name—hear ye him.

8 And it came to pass, as they understood they cast their eyes up again towards heaven; and behold, they saw a Man descending out of heaven; and he was clothed in a white robe; and he came down and stood in the midst of them; and the eyes of the whole multitude were turned upon him, and they durst not open their mouths, even one to another, and wist not what it meant, for they thought it was an angel that had appeared unto them.

9 And it came to pass that he stretched forth his hand and spake unto the people, saying:

10 Behold, I am Jesus Christ, whom the prophets testified shall come into the world.

11 And behold, I am the light and the life of the world; and I have drunk out of that bitter cup which the Father hath given me, and have glorified the Father in taking upon me the sins of the world, in the which I have suffered the will of the Father in all things from the beginning.

12 And it came to pass that when Jesus had spoken these words the whole multitude fell to the earth; for they remembered that it had been prophesied among them that Christ should show himself unto them after his ascension into heaven.

13 And it came to pass that the Lord spake unto them saying:

14 Arise and come forth unto me, that ye may thrust your hands into my side, and also that ye may feel the prints of the nails in my hands and in my feet, that ye may know that I am the God of Israel, and the God of the whole earth, and have been slain for the sins of the world.

15 And it came to pass that the multitude went forth, and thrust their hands into his side, and did feel the prints of the nails in his hands and in his feet; and this they did do, going forth one by one until they had all gone forth, and did see with their eyes and did feel with their hands, and did know of a surety and did bear record, that it was he, of whom it was written by the prophets, that should come.

16 And when they had all gone forth and had witnessed for themselves, they did cry out with one accord, saying:

17 Hosanna! Blessed be the name of the Most High God! And they did fall down at the feet of Jesus, and did worship him.

18 And it came to pass that he spake unto Nephi (for Nephi was among the multitude) and he commanded him that he should come forth.

19 And Nephi arose and went forth, and bowed himself before the Lord and did kiss his feet.

20 And the Lord commanded him that he should arise. And he arose and stood before him.

21 And the Lord said unto him: I give unto you power that ye shall baptize this people when I am again ascended into heaven.

22 And again the Lord called others, and said unto them likewise; and he gave unto them power to baptize. And he said unto them: On this wise shall

ye baptize; and there shall be no disputations among you.

23 Verily I say unto you, that whoso repenteth of his sins through your words, and desireth to be baptized in my name, on this wise shall ye baptize them—Behold, ye shall go down and stand in the water, and in my name shall ye baptize them.

24 And now behold, these are the words which ye shall say, calling them by name, saying:

25 Having authority given me of Jesus Christ, I baptize you in the name of the Father, and of the Son, and of the Holy Ghost. Amen.

26 And then shall ye immerse them in the water, and come forth again out of the water.

27 And after this manner shall ye baptize in my name; for behold, verily I say unto you, that the Father, and the Son, and the Holy Ghost are one; and I am in the Father, and the Father in me, and the Father and I are one.

28 And according as I have commanded you thus shall ye baptize. And there shall be no disputations among you, as there have hitherto been; neither shall there be disputations among you concerning the points of my doctrine, as there have hitherto been.

29 For verily, verily I say unto you, he that hath the spirit of contention is not of me, but is of the devil, who is the father of contention, and he stirreth up the hearts of men to contend with anger, one with another.

30 Behold, this is not my doctrine, to stir up the hearts of men with anger, one against another; but this is my doctrine, that such things should be done away.

31 Behold, verily, verily, I say unto you, I will declare unto you my doctrine.

32 And this is my doctrine, and it is the doctrine which the Father hath given unto me; and I bear record of the Father, and the Father beareth record of me, and the Holy Ghost beareth record of the Father and me; and I bear record that the Father commandeth all men, everywhere, to repent and believe in me.

33 And whoso believeth in me, and is baptized, the same shall be saved; and they are they who shall inherit the kingdom of God.

34 And whoso believeth not in me, and is not baptized, shall be damned.

35 Verily, verily, I say unto you, that this is my doctrine, and I bear record of it from the Father; and whoso believeth in me believeth in the Father also; and unto him will the Father bear record of me, for he will visit him with fire and with the Holy Ghost.

36 And thus will the Father bear record of me, and the Holy Ghost will bear record unto him of the Father and me; for the Father, and I, and the Holy Ghost are one.

37 And again I say unto you, ye must repent, and become as a little child, and be baptized in my name, or ye can in nowise receive these things.

38 And again I say unto you, ye must repent, and be baptized in my name, and become as a little child, or ye can in nowise inherit the kingdom of God.

39 Verily, verily, I say unto you, that this is my doctrine, and whoso buildeth upon this buildeth upon my rock, and the gates of hell shall not prevail against them.

40 And whoso shall declare more or less than this, and establish it for my doctrine, the same cometh of evil, and is not built upon my rock; but he buildeth upon a sandy foundation, and the gates of hell stand open to receive such when the floods come and the winds beat upon them.

41 Therefore, go forth unto this people, and declare the words which I have spoken, unto the ends of the earth.

CHAPTER 12

1 And it came to pass that when Jesus had spoken these words unto Nephi, and to those who had been called, (now the number of them who had been called, and received power and authority to baptize, was twelve) and behold, he stretched forth his hand unto the multitude, and cried unto them, saying: Blessed are ye if ye shall give heed unto the words of these twelve whom I have chosen from among you to minister unto you, and to be your servants; and unto them I have given power that they may baptize you with water; and after that ye are baptized with water, behold, I will baptize you with fire and with the Holy Ghost; therefore blessed are ye if ye shall believe in me and be baptized, after that ye have seen me and know that I am.

2 And again, more blessed are they who shall believe in your words because that ye shall testify that ye have seen me, and that ye know that I am. Yea, blessed are they who shall believe in your words, and come down into the depths of humility and be baptized, for they shall be visited with fire and with the Holy Ghost, and shall receive a remission of their sins.

3 Yea, blessed are the poor in spirit who come unto me, for theirs is the kingdom of heaven.

4 And again, blessed are all they that mourn, for they shall be comforted.

5 And blessed are the meek, for they shall inherit the earth.

6 And blessed are all they who do hunger and thirst after righteousness, for they shall be filled with the Holy Ghost.

7 And blessed are the merciful, for they shall obtain mercy.

8 And blessed are all the pure in heart, for they shall see God.

9 And blessed are all the peacemakers, for they shall be called the children of God.

10 And blessed are all they who are persecuted for my name's sake, for theirs is the kingdom of heaven.

11 And blessed are ye when men shall revile you and persecute, and shall say all manner of evil against you falsely, for my sake;

12 For ye shall have great joy and be exceedingly glad, for great shall be your reward in heaven; for so persecuted they the prophets who were before you.

13 Verily, verily, I say unto you, I give unto you to be the salt of the earth; but if the salt shall lose its savor wherewith shall the earth be salted? The salt shall be thenceforth good for nothing, but to be cast out and to be trodden under foot of men.

14 Verily, verily, I say unto you, I give unto you to be the light of this people. A city that is set on a hill cannot be hid.

15 Behold, do men light a candle and put it under a bushel? Nay, but on a candlestick, and it giveth light to all that are in the house;

16 Therefore let your light so shine before this people, that they may see your good works and glorify your Father who is in heaven.

17 Think not that I am come to destroy the law or the prophets. I am not come to destroy but to fulfil;

18 For verily I say unto you, one jot nor one tittle hath not passed away from the law, but in me it hath all been fulfilled.

19 And behold, I have given you the law and the commandments of my Father, that ye shall believe in me, and that ye shall repent of your sins, and

come unto me with a broken heart and a contrite spirit. Behold, ye have the commandments before you, and the law is fulfilled.

20 Therefore come unto me and be ye saved; for verily I say unto you, that except ye shall keep my commandments, which I have commanded you at this time, ye shall in no case enter into the kingdom of heaven.

21 Ye have heard that it hath been said by them of old time, and it is also written before you, that thou shalt not kill, and whosoever shall kill shall be in danger of the judgment of God;

22 But I say unto you, that whosoever is angry with his brother shall be in danger of his judgment. And whosoever shall say to his brother, Raca, shall be in danger of the council; and whosoever shall say, Thou fool, shall be in danger of hell fire.

23 Therefore, if ye shall come unto me, or shall desire to come unto me, and rememberest that thy brother hath aught against thee—

24 Go thy way unto thy brother, and first be reconciled to thy brother, and then come unto me with full purpose of heart, and I will receive you.

25 Agree with thine adversary quickly while thou art in the way with him, lest at any time he shall get thee, and thou shalt be cast into prison.

26 Verily, verily, I say unto thee, thou shalt by no means come out thence until thou hast paid the uttermost senine. And while ye are in prison can ye pay even one senine? Verily, verily, I say unto you, Nay.

27 Behold, it is written by them of old time, that thou shalt not commit adultery;

28 But I say unto you, that whosoever looketh on a woman, to lust after her, hath committed adultery already in his heart.

29 Behold, I give unto you a commandment, that

ye suffer none of these things to enter into your heart;

30 For it is better that ye should deny yourselves of these things, wherein ye will take up your cross, than that ye should be cast into hell.

31 It hath been written, that whosoever shall put away his wife, let him give her a writing of divorcement.

32 Verily, verily, I say unto you, that whosoever shall put away his wife, saving for the cause of fornication, causeth her to commit adultery; and whoso shall marry her who is divorced committeth adultery.

33 And again it is written, thou shalt not forswear thyself, but shalt perform unto the Lord thine oaths;

34 But verily, verily, I say unto you, swear not at all; neither by heaven, for it is God's throne;

35 Nor by the earth, for it is his footstool;

36 Neither shalt thou swear by thy head, because thou canst not make one hair black or white;

37 But let your communication be Yea, yea; Nay, nay; for whatsoever cometh of more than these is evil.

38 And behold, it is written, an eye for an eye, and a tooth for a tooth;

39 But I say unto you, that ye shall not resist evil, but whosoever shall smite thee on thy right cheek, turn to him the other also;

40 And if any man will sue thee at the law and take away thy coat, let him have thy cloak also;

41 And whosoever shall compel thee to go a mile, go with him twain.

42 Give to him that asketh thee, and from him that would borrow of thee turn thou not away.

43 And behold it is written also, that thou shalt love thy neighbor and hate thine enemy;

44 But behold I say unto you, love your enemies, bless them that curse you, do good to them that hate you, and pray for them who despitefully use you and persecute you;

45 That ye may be the children of your Father who is in heaven; for he maketh his sun to rise on the evil and on the good.

46 Therefore those things which were of old time, which were under the law, in me are all fulfilled.

47 Old things are done away, and all things have become new.

48 Therefore I would that ye should be perfect even as I, or your Father who is in heaven is perfect.

CHAPTER 17

1 Behold, now it came to pass that when Jesus had spoken these words he looked round about again on the multitude, and he said unto them: Behold, my time is at hand.

2 I perceive that ye are weak, that ye cannot understand all my words which I am commanded of the Father to speak unto you at this time.

3 Therefore, go ye unto your homes, and ponder upon the things which I have said, and ask of the Father, in my name, that ye may understand, and prepare your minds for the morrow, and I come unto you again.

4 But now I go unto the Father, and also to show myself unto the lost tribes of Israel, for they are not lost unto the Father, for he knoweth whither he hath taken them.

5 And it came to pass that when Jesus had thus spoken, he cast his eyes round about again on the multitude, and beheld they were in tears, and did look steadfastly upon him as if they would ask him to tarry a little longer with them.

6 And he said unto them: Behold, my bowels are filled with compassion towards you.

7 Have ye any that are sick among you? Bring them hither. Have ye any that are lame, or blind, or halt, or maimed, or leprous, or that are withered, or that are deaf, or that are afflicted in any manner? Bring them hither and I will heal them, for I have compassion upon you; my bowels are filled with mercy.

8 For I perceive that ye desire that I should show unto you what I have done unto your brethren at Jerusalem, for I see that your faith is sufficient that I should heal you.

9 And it came to pass that when he had thus spoken, all the multitude, with one accord, did go forth with their sick and their afflicted, and their lame, and with their blind, and with their dumb, and with all them that were afflicted in any manner; and he did heal them every one as they were brought forth unto him.

10 And they did all, both they who had been healed and they who were whole, bow down at his feet, and did worship him; and as many as could come for the multitude did kiss his feet, insomuch that they did bathe his feet with their tears.

11 And it came to pass that he commanded that their little children should be brought.

12 So they brought their little children and set them down upon the ground round about him, and Jesus stood in the midst; and the multitude gave way till they had all been brought unto him.

13 And it came to pass that when they had all been brought, and Jesus stood in the midst, he commanded the multitude that they should kneel down upon the ground.

14 And it came to pass that when they had knelt upon the ground, Jesus groaned within himself, and said: Father, I am troubled because of the wickedness of the people of the house of Israel.

15 And when he had said these words, he himself also knelt upon the earth; and behold he prayed unto the Father, and the things which he prayed cannot be written, and the multitude did bear record who heard him.

16 And after this manner do they bear record: The eye hath never seen, neither hath the ear heard, before, so great and marvelous things as we saw and heard Jesus speak unto the Father;

17 And no tongue can speak, neither can there be written by any man, neither can the hearts of men conceive so great and marvelous things as we both saw and heard Jesus speak; and no one can conceive of the joy which filled our souls at the time we heard him pray for us unto the Father.

18 And it came to pass that when Jesus had made an end of praying unto the Father, he arose; but so great was the joy of the multitude that they were overcome.

19 And it came to pass that Jesus spake unto them, and bade them arise.

20 And they arose from the earth, and he said unto them: Blessed are ye because of your faith. And now behold, my joy is full.

21 And when he had said these words, he wept, and the multitude bare record of it, and he took their little children, one by one, and blessed them, and prayed unto the Father for them.

22 And when he had done this he wept again;

23 And he spake unto the multitude, and said unto them: Behold your little ones.

24 And as they looked to behold they cast their eyes towards heaven, and they saw the heavens open, and they saw angels descending out of heaven as it

were in the midst of fire; and they came down and encircled those little ones about, and they were encircled about with fire; and the angels did minister unto them.

25 And the multitude did see and hear and bear record; and they know that their record is true for they all of them did see and hear, every man for himself; and they were in number about two thousand and five hundred souls; and they did consist of men, women, and children.

CHAPTER 18

1 And it came to pass that Jesus commanded his disciples that they should bring forth some bread and wine unto him.

2 And while they were gone for bread and wine, he commanded the multitude that they should sit themselves down upon the earth.

3 And when the disciples had come with bread and wine, he took of the bread and brake and blessed it; and he gave unto the disciples and commanded that they should eat.

4 And when they had eaten and were filled, he commanded that they should give unto the multitude.

5 And when the multitude had eaten and were filled, he said unto the disciples: Behold there shall one be ordained among you, and to him will I give power that he shall break bread and bless it and give it unto the people of my church, unto all those who shall believe and be baptized in my name.

6 And this shall ye always observe to do, even as I have done, even as I have broken bread and blessed it and given it unto you.

7 And this shall ye do in remembrance of my body, which I have shown unto you. And it shall be a testimony unto the Father that ye do always remember me. And if ye do always remember me ye shall have my Spirit to be with you.

8 And it came to pass that when he said these words, he commanded his disciples that they should take of the wine of the cup and drink of it, and that they should also give unto the multitude that they might drink of it.

9 And it came to pass that they did so, and did drink of it and were filled; and they gave unto the multitude, and they did drink, and they were filled.

10 And when the disciples had done this, Jesus said unto them: Blessed are ye for this thing which ye have done, for this is fulfilling my commandments, and this doth witness unto the Father that ye are willing to do that which I have commanded you.

11 And this shall ye always do to those who repent and are baptized in my name; and ye shall do it in remembrance of my blood, which I have shed for you, that ye may witness unto the Father that ye always remember me. And if ye do always remember me ye shall have my Spirit to be with you.

12 And I give unto you a commandment that ye shall do these things. And if ye shall always do these things blessed are ye, for ye are built upon my rock.

13 But whoso among you shall do more or less than these are not built upon my rock, but are built upon a sandy foundation; and when the rain descends, and the floods come, and the winds blow, and beat upon them, they shall fall, and the gates of hell are ready open to receive them.

14 Therefore blessed are ye if ye shall keep my commandments, which the Father hath commanded me that I should give unto you.

15 Verily, verily, I say unto you, ye must watch and pray always, lest ye be tempted by the devil, and ye be led away captive by him.

16 And as I have prayed among you even so shall ye pray in my church, among my people who do repent and are baptized in my name. Behold I am the light; I have set an example for you.

17 And it came to pass that when Jesus had spoken these words unto his disciples, he turned again unto the multitude and said unto them:

18 Behold, verily, verily, I say unto you, ye must watch and pray always lest ye enter into temptation; for Satan desireth to have you, that he may sift you as wheat.

19 Therefore ye must always pray unto the Father in my name;

20 And whatsoever ye shall ask the Father in my name, which is right, believing that ye shall receive, behold it shall be given unto you.

21 Pray in your families unto the Father, always in my name, that your wives and your children may be blessed.

22 And behold, ye shall meet together oft; and ye shall not forbid any man from coming unto you when ye shall meet together, but suffer them that they may come unto you and forbid them not;

23 But ye shall pray for them, and shall not cast them out; and if it so be that they come unto you oft ye shall pray for them unto the Father, in my name.

24 Therefore, hold up your light that it may shine unto the world. Behold I am the light which ye shall hold up—that which ye have seen me do. Behold ye see that I have prayed unto the Father, and ye all have witnessed.

25 And ye see that I have commanded that none of you should go away, but rather have commanded that ye should come unto me, that ye might feel and see; even so shall ye do unto the world; and whosoever breaketh this commandment suffereth himself to be led into temptation.

26 And now it came to pass that when Jesus had spoken these words, he turned his eyes again upon the disciples whom he had chosen, and said unto them:

27 Behold verily, verily, I say unto you, I give unto you another commandment, and then I must go unto my Father that I may fulfil other commandments which he hath given me.

28 And now behold, this is the commandment which I give unto you, that ye shall not suffer any one knowingly to partake of my flesh and blood unworthily, when ye shall minister it;

29 For whoso eateth and drinketh my flesh and blood unworthily eateth and drinketh damnation to his soul; therefore if ye know that a man is unworthy to eat and drink of my flesh and blood ye shall forbid him.

30 Nevertheless, ye shall not cast him out from among you, but ye shall minister unto him and shall pray for him unto the Father, in my name; and if it so be that he repenteth and is baptized in my name, then shall ye receive him, and shall minister unto him of my flesh and blood.

31 But if he repent not he shall not be numbered among my people, that he may not destroy my people, for behold I know my sheep, and they are numbered.

32 Nevertheless, ye shall not cast him out of your synagogues, or your places of worship, for unto such shall ye continue to minister; for ye know not but what they will return and repent, and come unto me with full purpose of heart, and I shall heal them; and ye shall be the means of bringing salvation unto them.

33 Therefore, keep these sayings which I have commanded you that ye come not under condemnation; for wo unto him whom the Father condemneth.

34 And I give you these commandments because of the disputations which have been among you. And blessed are ye if ye have no disputations among you.

35 And now I go unto the Father, because it is expedient that I should go unto the Father for your sakes.

36 And it came to pass that when Jesus had made an end of these sayings, he touched with his hand the disciples whom he had chosen, one by one, even until he had touched them all, and spake unto them as he touched them.

37 And the multitude heard not the words which he spake, therefore they did not bear record; but the disciples bare record that he gave them power to give the Holy Ghost. And I will show unto you hereafter that this record is true.

38 And it came to pass that when Jesus had touched them all, there came a cloud and overshadowed the multitude that they could not see Jesus.

39 And while they were overshadowed he departed from them, and ascended into heaven. And the disciples saw and did bear record that he ascended again into heaven.

CHAPTER 19

1 And now it came to pass that when Jesus had ascended into heaven, the multitude did disperse, and every man did take his wife and his children and did return to his own home.

2 And it was noised abroad among the people immediately, before it was yet dark, that the multitude had seen Jesus, and that he had ministered unto them, and that he would also show himself on the morrow unto the multitude.

3 Yea, and even all the night it was noised abroad concerning Jesus; and insomuch did they send forth unto the people that there were many, yea, an exceedingly great number, did labor exceedingly all that night, that they might be on the morrow in the place where Jesus should show himself unto the multitude.

4 And it came to pass that on the morrow, when the multitude was gathered together, behold, Nephi and his brother whom he had raised from the dead, whose name was Timothy, and also his son, whose name was Jonas, and also Mathoni, and Mathonihah, his brother, and Kumen, and Kumenonhi, and Jeremiah, and Shemnon, and Jonas, and Zedekiah, and Isaiah—now these were the names of the disciples whom Jesus had chosen—and it came to pass that they went forth and stood in the midst of the multitude.

5 And behold, the multitude was so great that they did cause that they should be separated into twelve bodies.

6 And the twelve did teach the multitude; and behold, they did cause that the multitude should kneel down upon the face of the earth, and should pray unto the Father in the name of Jesus.

7 And the disciples did pray unto the Father also in the name of Jesus. And it came to pass that they arose and ministered unto the people.

8 And when they had ministered those same words which Jesus had spoken—nothing varying from the words which Jesus had spoken—behold, they knelt again and prayed to the Father in the name of Jesus.

9 And they did pray for that which they most desired; and they desired that the Holy Ghost should be given unto them.

10 And when they had thus prayed they went down unto the water's edge, and the multitude followed them.

11 And it came to pass that Nephi went down into the water and was baptized.

12 And he came up out of the water and began to baptize. And he baptized all those whom Jesus had chosen.

13 And it came to pass when they were all baptized and had come up out of the water, the Holy Ghost did fall upon them, and they were filled with the Holy Ghost and with fire.

14 And behold, they were encircled about as if it were by fire; and it came down from heaven, and the multitude did witness it, and did bear record; and angels did come down out of heaven and did minister unto them.

15 And it came to pass that while the angels were ministering unto the disciples, behold, Jesus came and stood in the midst and ministered unto them.

16 And it came to pass that he spake unto the multitude, and commanded them that they should kneel down again upon the earth, and also that his disciples should kneel down upon the earth.

17 And it came to pass that when they had all knelt down upon the earth, he commanded his disciples that they should pray.

18 And behold, they began to pray; and they did pray unto Jesus, calling him their Lord and their God.

19 And it came to pass that Jesus departed out of the midst of them, and went a little way off from them and bowed himself to the earth, and he said:

20 Father, I thank thee that thou hast given the Holy Ghost unto these whom I have chosen; and it is because of their belief in me that I have chosen them out of the world.

21 Father, I pray thee that thou wilt give the Holy Ghost unto all them that shall believe in their words.

22 Father, thou hast given them the Holy Ghost because they believe in me; and thou seest that they believe in me because thou hearest them, and they pray unto me; and they pray unto me because I am with them.

23 And now Father, I pray unto thee for them, and also for all those who shall believe on their words, that they may believe in me, that I may be in them as thou, Father, art in me, that we may be one.

24 And it came to pass that when Jesus had thus prayed unto the Father, he came unto his disciples, and behold, they did still continue, without ceasing, to pray unto him; and they did not multiply many words, for it was given unto them what they should pray, and they were filled with desire.

25 And it came to pass that Jesus blessed them as they did pray unto him; and his countenance did smile upon them, and the light of his countenance did shine upon them, and behold they were as white as the countenance and also the garments of Jesus; and behold the whiteness thereof did exceed all the whiteness, yea, even there could be nothing upon earth so white as the whiteness thereof.

26 And Jesus said unto them: Pray on; nevertheless they did not cease to pray.

27 And he turned from them again, and went a little way off and bowed himself to the earth; and he prayed again unto the Father, saying:

28 Father, I thank thee that thou hast purified those whom I have chosen, because of their faith, and I pray for them, and also for them who shall believe on their words, that they may be purified in me, through faith on their words, even as they are purified in me.

29 Father, I pray not for the world, but for those whom thou hast given me out of the world, because of their faith, that they may be purified in me, that I may be in them as thou, Father, art in me, that we may be one, that I may be glorified in them.

30 And when Jesus had spoken these words he came again unto his disciples; and behold they did pray steadfastly, without ceasing, unto him; and he did smile upon them again; and behold they were white, even as Jesus.

31 And it came to pass that he went again a little way off and prayed unto the Father;

32 And tongue cannot speak the words which he prayed, neither can be written by man the words which he prayed.

33 And the multitude did hear and do bear record; and their hearts were open and they did understand in their hearts the words which he prayed.

34 Nevertheless, so great and marvelous were the words which he prayed that they cannot be written, neither can they be uttered by man.

35 And it came to pass that when Jesus had made an end of praying he came again to the disciples, and said unto them: So great faith have I never seen among all the Jews; wherefore I could not show unto them so great miracles, because of their unbelief.

36 Verily I say unto you, there are none of them that have seen so great things as ye have seen; neither have they heard so great things as ye have heard.

Acknowledgments

Cameron Trejo is the master storyteller who brings all the elements together in this project. Thank you, Cameron, for the patience to listen and watch. Thank you for the wisdom to interpret what was going on. And thank you for the talent to make it all come together. Now go and get some sleep.

Robert Allen's portrayal of the Savior has been respectful and filled with a worshipful humbleness. Thank you for giving the participants license to imagine. Thank you for living as needed.

Together Clyde Bawden and Jason Barney have lifted the images to new heights with their musical score of *Another Testament*. Their music lifts and inspires me throughout the entire creative process. Their dedication to making passionate music that is relevant and engaging has given everyone energy to work.

The patience of my wife and children (Tara, Mark III, Bowan, Ava Liv, and the almost-here baby) is much appreciated. Thank you for giving me a little extra time to read and travel. You inspire me to try and live up to my work. The lessons that I've learned by working on this project have deepened my love for each of you.

Mark Sr. and Jerri Mabry for your consistent support and love. Thanks for the set of scriptures with my name on them that you gave me when I was eight. Thank you for the mission. Thank you for raising me in an environment that let me grow up believing that it could all be true.

This project would have been poorer without Steve Porter's relentless push and organization. His passion for the area and subject added much polish to the project. Thank you for the insight and travels. Thank you for being picky when I wasn't. Thank you for showing me what happens when you shut the engine off in an airplane and for the forty-five minute speech on the east wilderness.

Marlane Porter's ability to process information at incredible speeds and her ability to make fantastic costumes blended perfectly with Becky McMeen's raw artistic talent. The costumes are a highlight of these images. For those that look closely, they are also a deep teaching tool. Thank you for the prayer and sweat you put into the design and production of these pieces.

In Memory of Ralph Charles Trejo (1915–2009) and Talmage Dennis Barney (1946–2009)

CREDITS

COSTUMES AND PROPS

Costume Designer and Producer: Marlane Porter

Costume Designer and Co-Producer: Becky McMeen

Costume Production: Norine Allen, Jayme Bawden, Samantha Baxter, Tangie Baxter, Dana Burnett, Betty Brown, Renita Calton, Molly DeCrow, Joan Glenn, Paige Glenn, ElDeane Heugly, Michelle Hollis, Julia Jones, Debbie Lemieux, Alissa Lines, Permilia Lucia, Tara Mabry, Becky McMeen, Amanda Porter, Catie Porter, Liz Porter, Marlane Porter, Tara Porter, Carolyn Schnepf, Kelli Skousen, Cindy Spencer, Rebecca Willcox

Christ's Robe #1: Barb Layton

Christ's Robe #2: Marlane Porter, Becky McMeen

Costume and Hairstyling (on location): Norine Allen, Dani Birchall, Kadence Eaton, Diane Heyman, Chelsee Hunt, Jerri Mabry, Tara Mabry, Becky McMeen, Amanda Porter, Catie Porter, Liz Porter, Marlane Porter, Rechelle Trejo

Lead Hair Stylist: Chelsee Hunt

Props: Parker Merrill, R.C. Merrill Studios, Sterling Leavitt (plates), Rick Tyler (plates)

Costume/Post Production/Angel Shoot Facilities provided by Clyde and Jayme Bawden

PHOTOGRAPHY

Production Manager: Steve Porter

Behind the Scenes Photography: Dixie Waters

1st Assistant: Jake Bawden

Photography Assistants (on location): Clyde Bawden, Jason Barney, Kim Eaton, Ray Heyman, Taylor Heyman, Mark Mabry Sr., Don Porter, Lee Porter

Photography Assistants and help for Angels Photo Shoot: Gary Cornia, Travis Fenn, Ava Liv Mabry (for the trampoline), Bowan Mabry, Marko Mabry, Ryan Mortensen, Holden Williams, Jarrett Williams

POSTPRODUCTION

Primary Illustrator and Effects Artist: Todd Sheridan

Retouch Artists: Dee Lafferty, Matt McLelland, Todd Sheridan, Dixie Waters

Exhibit Framing and Design: Rob Brinton/Matage Custom Framing

Location Management and Accommodations: Jorge Molanphy & Frank Molanphy

Copan Hotel Provided by: Hotel Madrugada (www.hotelmadrugada.com)

FILM CREW

Production

Jared Foster—Cameraman

Cameron Trejo—Producer/Director/Camera

Casey Trejo—Boom Operator/Prod. Assistant

Rechelle Trejo—Assistant Producer

Postproduction

Todd Sheridan—Motion Graphics Artist

Cameron Trejo—Editor

Interviews

Dr. Dennis Deaton

Mark Mabry

Camille Fronk Olson

Dr. John C. Welch

Cast Members

Jose Antonio Amador, Marta Dias Basqulb, Marco Antonio Bonilla, Kisakka Bonilla, Krizzia Bonilla, Joshua Bonilla, Kerry Bonilla, Jirod Bonilla, Steven Budd, Linda Abigail Budd, Michael Jeremy Budd, Sariah Nicole Budd, Danny Budd, Spencer Budd, Thamia Budd, Jaqueline Chiu, Blanca Rosa Chiu, Angie Sayure Galindo Chiu, Lorena Galindo Chiu, Karla Balindo Chiu, Nahomy Balindo Chiu, Carlos A. Cuellar, Reina Idalia de Ferrera, Mireya da Bonilla, Adriana Gonzales De Manley, Alejandrina Melgar Dubon, Hilda Esperanza, Concepcion Esquivel, Elder Noe Ferrara, Edvin Ariel Ferrara, Nilda Hazel GoTay Frarizua, Yolan Amador Garcia, Pamela Ivonne Amador Garcia, Larry Amador Garcia, Bessy Olimpia Perdome Garcia, Jesus Alberto Garcia, Oscar Avila Gonzales, Josue Hernandez GoTay, Elder Basilio Guerra, Denise Jose Aguilar Helgar, Juana Ranos Hernandez, Julian Hernandez, Jose Donaldo Interiano, David B. Koenig, Cody Koenig, Otoniel Manley, Adriana Manley, Jose Antonio Amador Martinez, Maria Lordes Martinez, Jose Ramon Mejia, Amanda Orbelina Mejia, Christian Josue Mejia, Astrid Valerie Mejia, Nefi Jose Mejia, Yeisi Larissa Mejia, Digna Esmeralda Mejia, Irma Lorena Mevia Melgar, Luis Omar Melora, Jorge Francisco Molanphy, Liza Nadine Molanphy, Mateo Molanphy, Natalia Molanphy, Sofia Molanphy, David Alejandro Aguilar Moncada, Vidorra Alejandro Aguilar Moncada, Hose Roberto Aguilar Moncada, Francisco Fores Paz, Bessy Paola Melora Perdomo, Ezra Ammon Melora Perdomo, Hyrum Omar Melora Perdomo, Owen Ezra Melora Perdomo, Manuel Santos Perez, Yadira Estela Moncada Ponce, Axell Eduardo Rios, Karla Esther Fonseca Rivas, Gladys Esther Rivas, Kiomy Millan Sosa, Aylon Yarli Sosa, Karlo Patricia Vega, Mario Alexander Vega, Manuel Alberto Vega, Andres A. Thomas Zapota

Angels

Katie Aiona, Kati Araiza, Tainui Berryman, Hannah Brown, Rosanna Buckmister, Shauni Dyar, Ryan Dyches Jr., Charlie Fahina, Chelsea Foster, Paige Glenn, Kenny Golladay, Marcelo Gomes, Adam Gonzales, Jordana Gordic, Anthony Gruninger, Garrette Gruninger, Hudson Helm, Jackson Helm, Mazie Hoffman, Beth Jabe, Seth Lopez, Mariah Martinsen, Sosaia Mataele, Jennifer McClelland, Angela Milne, Mark Nielsen, Rex Nielson, Chelsi Nye, Rose Perez, Rachelle Perez, Catie Porter, Sara Pringle, Karissa Sherwood, Cami Shreeve, Jake Shreeve, Robert Skousen, Jacqueline Smith, Elisa Soto, Chad Tialino, Jared Whaler, Jamie Willcox, Candice Woods

Special Thanks

The Copan Ruins for the beautiful location and extra help that made the entire shoot possible.

Brigham Young University Museum of the Arts Center

The Olson family and the Bawden family for allowing us to shoot in their homes.

LeGrand L. Baker

Karen Gruninger

Dr. John Sorensen

Frank Molanphy (for providing heavy gear for our equipment in Honduras!)

Jerry Trejo

Keith and Audrey Ryan for watching the kids and allowing Tara to enjoy this adventure.

Mom and Dad and my seven sisters for the continued love and support.

Clyde and Jayme for the retouching sanctuary.

Deseret Book Company: Sophie Barth, Leigh Dethman, Sheri Dew, Jana Erickson, Richard Erickson, Tonya Facemyer, Gail Halladay, Nathan Jarvis, Lisa Mangum, Lani Rush, Chris Schoebinger, Anne Sheffield, Sheryl Dickert Smith, Heidi Taylor, Heather Ward, Boyd Ware